EAST SUS
WALKS

G000055310

BRIGHTON, EASTBOURNE AND LEWES AREA

Sandy Hernu

S.B. Publications

**For my husband, Jeffrey,
with love**

First published in 1993 by S.B. Publications
c/o 19 Grove Road, Seaford, East Sussex BN25 1TP

Reprinted 1994
Reprinted 1996

ISBN 1 85770 045 7

Typeset and printed by Island Press Ltd, 01323 490222 UK

CONTENTS

Front Cover: *Telscombe Village*
Back Cover: *Barcombe Mills*
Title Page: *'Jasper', the author's dog*

ACKNOWLEDGEMENTS

I would like to thank the late Mac McCarthy for all his help and letting me have access to his notes on some of the many walks that he has done in the past.

All illustrations by the author.

THE AUTHOR

Brought up and having lived in Sussex for many years, Sandy Hernu shares her love of both, the countryside and history, by writing the first, of what is hoped to be, a series of books about Sussex.

Sandy, together with her husband, own and run The Alfriston Heritage Centre and Blacksmiths' Museum in Alfriston, East Sussex.

By the same author:-
    Exploring Alfriston and the Cuckmere Valley (1992)

INTRODUCING EAST SUSSEX

Both East and West Sussex are scenically beautiful. Apart from delightful countryside, they both have the added attractions of coastal shores, easy reach of London and proximity to Europe. This adds up to a very desirable area, either to live in, stay in or just to visit for the day or weekend.

Both counties have the wide backbone of the South Downs running across the greater part of them. From Beachy Head, near Eastbourne, to Midhurst, near the Hampshire border. The well known walk, the South Downs Way, passes through villages, along country lanes and deep into the heart of the downland. You would truly know Sussex after trekking those glorious eighty-six miles.

The boundaries of East Sussex start from Brighton and Hove in the west, finishing at Rye and Camber in the east and stretching beyond Ashdown Forest to the north. It has much to offer. That superb downland weald hides a jewel around every corner. Be it winding rivers or green meadows, picturesque villages steeped in history, Norman churches, their square flint facades blending beautifully with the rural surroundings. Sheer chalk white cliffs and the sea, sometimes grey or green, sometimes blue. Historic towns, or quiet lanes. The alluring attributes of East Sussex could be extolled for ever.

These circular walks or rambles encompass all of those things mentioned. They take in some history, indicate the points of interest and captivate the natural charm of the area. Obviously it is possible to just do part of them at any one time, but the majority are planned to take, at a leisurely pace, about half a day including a stop for lunch or tea.

The three main towns in the surrounding landscape are Brighton, Lewes and Eastbourne of which, Brighton is the largest. Once it was the tiny fishing village of Brighthelmstone, until the Prince Regent, in the 1780's, bought a house there, then had it rebuilt and remodelled into the flamboyant, fantastic Royal Pavilion. No longer was Brighthelmstone a fishing village. It became Brighton, achieved fame and the graceful Regency town with beautiful terraced houses had been born. It was fashionable, not only because of the infamous Prince Regent, but because it was suddenly considered healthy to "take the sea air" and indulge in sea bathing. Unfortunately,

Brighton like so many places has grown enormously. It is often known as the "little London by the sea". This is partially due to its excellent selection of theatres, cinemas, shops and restaurants. The lovely, old and intimate area of The Lanes offer an intriguing and confusing choice of antique or jewellery shops. There are four miles of promenade and two piers, although sadly, one has fallen into disrepair. The other, however, in the last few years has been renovated and it is pleasing to see this unique example of Victorian architecture restored and used once more.

Eastbourne, also a coastal resort, lies east of Beachy Head. Its buildings are mainly late Victorian or early Edwardian and it developed under the protection of the Dukes of Devonshire. The organized planning of the town properties, the promenade with its attractive hotels and gardens, bandstand and pier all show a great deal of thought, design and good taste. Like Brighton it has a variety of shops, theatres and restaurants.

Eastbourne is also ideally situated for exploring not only the spectacular countryside to the west but the area to the east. Known as 1066 Country, it was here, at Pevensey, near Eastbourne, that William of Normandy landed in 1066 and subsequently fought and won the most famous battle in history — The Battle of Hastings. A new era in England was about to begin and the Norman victors lost no time in claiming and using their newly acquired land. They built castles, abbeys, priories and churches, many we can still see today. One such castle was built at Lewes by the noble William de Warenne, a follower of William the Conqueror. It was rebuilt in stone in the 12th century and in 1264 after the Battle of Lewes, when King Henry III was defeated by Simon de Montfort, two octagonal towers were added. The towers and part of the castle still remain. Sited on huge man-made mounds, it provides a distinctive landmark for Lewes and together with the Barbican and the Keep can be visited throughout the year.

The ancient county town of Lewes has a southerly aspect. To the east lie the Downs of Cliffe Hill, Saxon Down and Mount Caburn, all of which bear evidence of Roman and pre-Roman occupation. The River Ouse that flows through the town has provided, over the years, an important means of transportation, especially during the eighteenth century, when Lewes became a prosperous community. Goods were brought up-river from Newhaven to the old warehouses that lined the river banks at Cliffe High Street. Some of them are still there, converted of course for a different use now.

The town properties stem from various eras although the Georgian influence is fairly predominant. Some of the houses exhibit a Georgian frontage but are much older within. Several interesting buildings include:- Shelleys Hotel, residence of the Shelley family; Anne of Cleeves House, given to Henry VIII's fourth wife as part of the divorce settlement; Southover Grange, the fifteenth century Bull House, just near the steep, cobbled Keere Street. There is certainly more than enough to keep the visitor satisfied.

Finally, the rural landscape whose history goes back a great deal further than any town or village, back way beyond the realms of our imagination and where these walks take place. Hopefully, this book will not only enable you to explore new terrain and appreciate the scenery, it will also help you dwell a little on the past, learn a little about the countryside, think a little about the future preservation of our heritage and above all, enjoy Sussex.

EAST SUSSEX

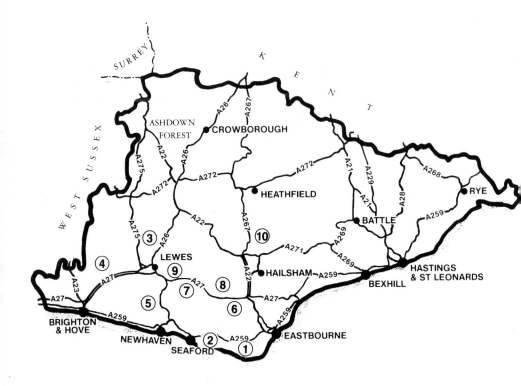

LOCATION OF WALKS

1. Crowlink
2. Cuckmere Haven
3. Barcombe Mills
4. Ditchling Beacon
5. Rodmell and Telscombe
6. Jevington and Wilmington
7. Firle
8. Arlington
9. Glynde and Mount Caburn
10. The Cuckoo Line

KEY TO MAPS

1. All maps are not entirely to scale.

2. All Points of Interest are underlined on the maps.

3. All numbers on the maps indicate route directions (see text as well).

4. (P) denotes a parking place.

5. Railways are marked by a crossed line.

Walk 1

CROWLINK

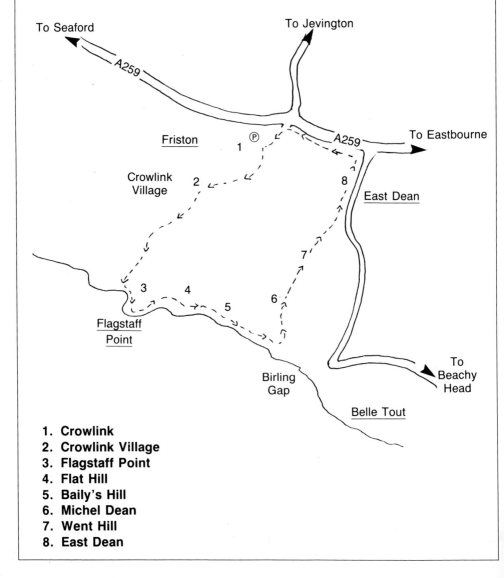

1. **Crowlink**
2. **Crowlink Village**
3. **Flagstaff Point**
4. **Flat Hill**
5. **Baily's Hill**
6. **Michel Dean**
7. **Went Hill**
8. **East Dean**

Walk 1

CROWLINK

Distance	Approx. 5 miles.
Route	Crowlink — Crowlink Village — Flagstaff Point — Flat Hill — Baily's Hill — Michel Dean — Went Hill — East Dean — Crowlink.
Maps	O/S Pathfinder 1324.
Start/Parking	Turn left to Crowlink, off the A259 from Eastbourne, by Friston Church. A short unmade track leads to a parking area.
Public Transport	Southdown Buses, 712.
Conditions	A very scenic walk, but fairly strenuous as there are quite a lot of steep, uphill areas along the cliff tops. Usually dry underfoot as it crosses downland. It can be windy on the coastline. There are also large flocks of sheep grazing, so it is necessary to keep dogs on a lead.
Refreshments	The Tiger Inn, East Dean.

Passing between the picturesque Friston Church and a pond frequently strewn with water iris and lilies in the summer, one is unprepared for the sudden change in scenery when rounding the corner. Suddenly, there is a wide open expanse of downland, with the sea in the distance, inviting on a good day, forbidding on a rough one. Park the car, get out, breathe the clear air and look long and long at the spectacular scenery before you, the silence broken only by the cry of the seagulls.

It is therefore a surprise when, after following a concrete path, that seems somewhat out of keeping with this rural area, you come across Crowlink

Village, nestling out of sight, in the valley. The properties look soft and mellow, their old clay tiles partially covered with lichen, the gardens where snowdrops, crocuses and primroses stray into the short downland turf and the shrubs blend into the hillside. It is so very pretty and will make a lasting impression.

Crowlink Village (Hamlet).

Stroll on now, down the valley towards the sea. Here flocks of sheep graze and the slopes are thick with elder and gorse. These in turn are undermined by rabbit burrows, the rabbits making a labyrinth of the chalky soil and the valley providing them with a playground. On reaching the cliff tops, the wind picks up. No longer do you stroll but walk quickly marvelling at the seascape, which on a clear day, would almost make one believe you could see France.

On towards Birling Gap, not a particularly pretty place. It has a salty, slightly decrepid feeling about it, almost as though it has been left over from a long forgotten film set. However, there are steps down to a shingle beach, where the swimming is very good. A more sheltered stretch now, back to the attractive village of East Dean, which has a lovely old pub on the Green. Sitting outside, with a drink, in the early evening sun, or indeed at any time, is a very pleasant experience before finally setting off back to Crowlink.

Route Directions

Leave the Car Park at Crowlink (1) by the gate at the end and follow the concrete road down the hill. This area can be quite busy at the weekends. The unusual Crowlink Village (2) is at the bottom of the hill. Take the dirt track through the village to the gate at the end. Now keep to the edge of the field until the next gate that leads into the valley, called Gap Bottom. Here you will find an example of an old downland dewpond. Note Gayles Farm up on the right in a commanding position of the surrounding scenery. When you reach the sea turn left along the cliffs. The first climb up is Flagstaff Brow. This leads to a protruding headland with wonderful views, known as Flagstaff Point (3). The Sarsen stone, erected in 1926, is on this point.

Now follow the well trodden tracks by man, sheep and rabbits alike, along the cliff tops. First to Flat Hill (4), then down, up to Baily's Hill (5), this is a steep climb, and on to Michel Dene. Above Michel Dene (6), after the fourth climb up, turn left. The seaside hamlet of Birling Gap, which you can just see, in the valley, will be on your right. I'm sure its coastguard cottages must be able to tell many a tale of smuggling.

Make for the gate, facing inland, along the top of the cliffs, then follow the fence until the next gate. Turn left, take the uphill track northwards and past a barn with a particularly brightly painted corrugated roof. This is Went Hill (7). Leave the track now and keeping the scrubland immediately on your right, take the next right hand path. This is steep and narrow and descends through woodland. It can also be very easy to miss, so watch out for it carefully. A sheltered seat is positioned here so one can enjoy the lovely southerly views towards Beachy Head. Now pass through a field and then an iron gate leading into East Dean (8). Go by the old cottages and Bakehouse until reaching the village green and Tiger Inn. Cross the green and take the signed footpath opposite which leads back to Friston Church and the car park at Crowlink.

Points of Interest

Friston

The name Friston is possibly derived from that of the Saxon landowner "Fritha". In those remote days an area of land was known as a "Tun". It would therefore, have been "Fritha's Tun". The church is probably Norman and although altered or added to over the centuries, it retains a simplicity that, coupled with its setting, make it one of the most attractive. The area of Friston west of the car park was requisitioned by the RAF in 1940 as an emergency landing ground. Not only did damaged aircraft use it throughout the war but in 1943 Friston airfield acquired its own squadron of Spitfires. It is somewhat hard to imagine this peaceful area alive with wartime activity.

Flagstaff Point

This prominent headland, which is part of the cliffs named "The Seven Sisters" gives splendid views along the coast to Cuckmere Haven and Seaford Head in the West. In the East lies the famous "suicide cliff", Beachy Head.

The Sarsen Stone positioned here was erected by the Society of Sussex Downsmen in 1926. It was in appreciation of the donation by William Charles Campbell towards the purchase of The Seven Sisters for the enjoyment of the nation.

Flagstaff Point.

Belle Tout

The old lighthouse of Belle Tout can be seen in the east from Flagstaff Point. Perched high on the cliff this hundred and fifty year old lighthouse is now a part of the adjoining residence. Although it has a strategic position overlooking Beachy Head, sea mists frequently enveloped it and a new light-house, which operates automatically, had to be built at the foot of the cliffs.

East Dean

The old part of East Dean is typical of a downland village. Flint built cottages and houses, most of which, during their former years, had various trades plied from them. The names of the cottages often speak for themselves, such as, The Old Bakehouse, The Schoolhouse and The Forge.

Unfortunately, during the last forty years, East Dean has expanded and now it joins the estates of Friston. However, the old part clustered around the Village Green and The Tiger Inn is charming. According to legend, the smugglers who landed at Birling Gap, used The Tiger Inn as a meeting place or headquarters. A landmark for many miles around used to be the windmill, sited just above East Dean on the Downs. It was rebuilt in 1826, having been blown down in a gale two years earlier. Sadly, it was blown down yet again, exactly one hundred years later and in similar circumstances. This time it was not rebuilt.

The Tiger Inn, East Dean.

Walk 2

CUCKMERE HAVEN

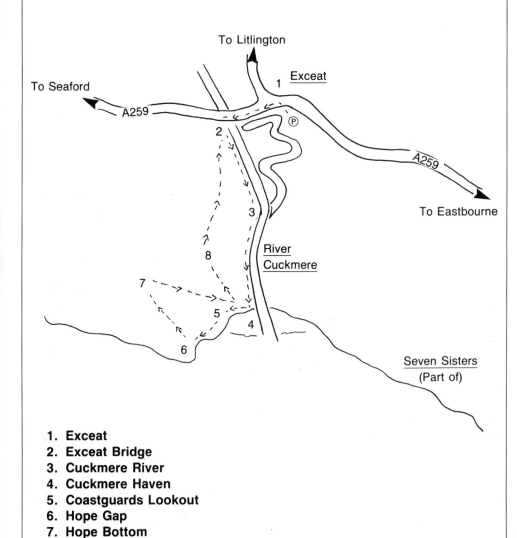

1. **Exceat**
2. **Exceat Bridge**
3. **Cuckmere River**
4. **Cuckmere Haven**
5. **Coastguards Lookout**
6. **Hope Gap**
7. **Hope Bottom**
8. **Outbrook Bank**

Walk 2

CUCKMERE HAVEN

Distance	Approx. 4 miles.
Route	Exceat — Exceat Bridge — Cuckmere River — Cuckmere Haven — Coastguards Lookout — Hope Gap — Hope Bottom — Outbrook Bank — Exceat.
Maps	O/S Pathfinder 1324.
Start/Parking	Exceat Car Park. On the left at the bottom of a hill leading down to the Cuckmere Valley from Eastbourne on the A259.
Public Transport	Southdown Buses, 712. Cuckmere Community Bus.
Conditions	Can sometimes be muddy along the towpath by the Cuckmere River. Otherwise an easy walk with one or two gentle ascents.
Refreshments	Exceat Farmhouse and the Golden Galleon. Both at Exceat but situated either side of the valley on the A259.

I feel that this particular walk should really be called "Where Smugglers Walked", because the route we take today is the one they used many, many years ago. Smuggling was rife along this coastline, due to its proximity to France. Cuckmere Haven was of course ideal with its river and inlets providing natural waterways for the transportation and hiding of goods. Even the prominent south-easterly position of the coastguard cottages overlooking the river mouth did not deter the smuggling fraternity. There were several landing sites between Newhaven and

Eastbourne for bringing in contraband, two of which, Cuckmere Haven and Hope Gap, you will pass on this walk.

As well as the usual goods being smuggled in, such as tea, coffee, rum, brandy, tobacco, lace and silks, goods were smuggled out. This was known as "owling", the illegal exporting of wool. The Sussex fleeces were highly prized in Europe.

Now more than a hundred and fifty years later, the whole area of the lower Cuckmere makes up "The Seven Sisters Country Park", owned and managed by the East Sussex County Council. On the western headland, adjacent to the Coastguard Cottages, lies Seaford Head Nature Reserve.

The "Lagoon", as it is called, at Exceat, is a shallow construction to enable wading birds to use it for feeding. The river, its banks, the meadows and scrubland provide nesting and feeding grounds for both resident and migrating birds. These include various species of ducks and gulls, swans, herons, redshank, plovers, sandpipers, avocet, cormorants and grebes.

The rising cliffs from Cuckmere Haven have showy outcrops of gorse, elder, blackthorn, hawthorn and dog roses growing in sheltered corners and the flocks of sheep grazing peacefully on the surrounding downland enhance an idyllic picture of this very beautiful area.

Swans nesting in the Cuckmere Valley.

Route Directions

From the Car Park at Exceat (1) turn left and follow the road until you get to Exceat Bridge (2). Cross the bridge and turn left into the Car Park of the Golden Galleon. At the end is a gateway and stile. Cross the stile and take the grass track until the next gateway. Turn left here and head towards the Cuckmere River (3). When you reach the river, stay on the towpath which turns right. You will now be in the midst of some lovely scenery. It is also worthwhile to bring binoculars, so one can study the various water birds a little more closely.

Continue with the river on the left until you reach the sea at Cuckmere Haven (4), once a landing site for smuggling. Turn right and walk across the beach and up to the old Coastguards Cottages (5), follow the track past them, then bear left across the grassy cliff tops. Follow the line of the cliffs, not too near the edge as chalk can crumble very easily. After about half a mile, there is an incline leading into a valley. Here there are steep steps leading down to a rocky cove which is called Hope Gap (6), another landing site for smugglers' contraband. On reaching the steps turn right up Hope Bottom (7). Notice the mass of yellow gorse everywhere. There always seems to be some gorse, somewhere in Hope Bottom, that is in bloom throughout the year. Perhaps because it is very sheltered.

At the top of the valley, turn right along the grit track which goes down past the Coastguard Cottages again. On this part of the walk, you will be rewarded with the most photographed and painted view in East Sussex, Cuckmere Haven and The Seven Sisters. It really is a splendid sight. At the bottom of the slope, before reaching the beach, turn sharp left along the path that hugs the western side of Cuckmere Haven, keeping the river on the right. This is Outbrook Bank (8). Continue for about a mile and a quarter until reaching the Golden Galleon Car Park again. The return route is really very easy to follow. Turn right to go back to Exceat.

Points of Interest

Exceat

In the 13th century the thriving village of Exceat, which included a church, was sited on the Downs just above what is now the Car Park. In 1332 the tax returns indicate a population of almost a hundred. However, frequent raids by the French and finally, the Black Death, caused it to sink into decline and by 1528, with only one householder left it was amalgamated with West Dean.

The 18th century barns, opposite the car park, have been beautifully restored. One barn provides a Visitor Centre with information on the area and the remaining barns have been converted to hold a living natural history exhibition.

The River Cuckmere

The Cuckmere is one of the smaller Sussex rivers being only about twenty miles long. It has two sources, one at Possingworth and one near Heathfield. Both places are situated in the High Weald which is about five hundred feet above sea level, so the river descends considerably before it reaches the sea at Cuckmere Haven.

It journeys through some of the most picturesque countryside which once echoed to the sounds of the Wealden iron industry. It flows past the old mills at Hellingly and Horsebridge, past the moated sites of Michelham and Sessingham and then through the lovely unspoilt Cuckmere Valley.

The natural course of the river was to follow the Meanders, which are a major feature of this area. However, in 1846 in order to reduce the flooding, the river was "canalized" or straightened south from Exceat Bridge.

The Seven Sisters

Looking eastwards, the stretch of cliffs called The Seven Sisters lies between Cuckmere Haven and Eastbourne. It is one of the finest stretches of coastal scenery in England and you will not find a better view of it, than from just above the old Coastguard Cottages.

The whole area, as far as you can see, both east and west, has been acquired by local authorities or The National Trust and has been designated as an area of outstanding natural beauty. The cliffs have also witnessed many tragedies, for although this coastline is beautiful it can also be treacherous in bad weather. Records indicate that since 1563, there have been more than twenty-five shipwrecks between The Seven Sisters and Cuckmere Haven.

The Seven Sisters.

The Golden Galleon, Exceat.

Walk 3

BARCOMBE MILLS

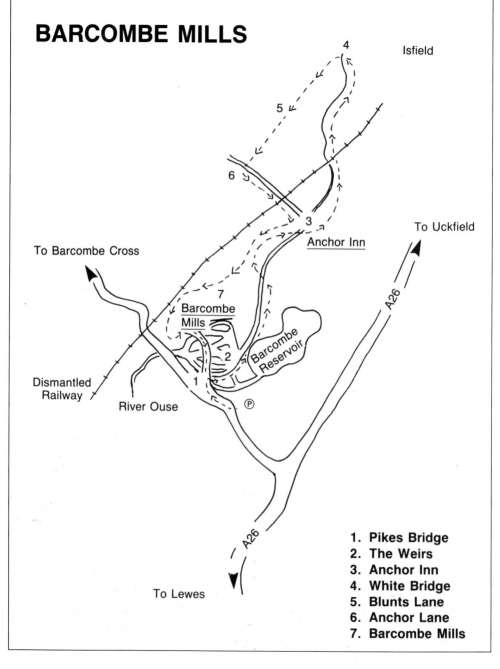

1. Pikes Bridge
2. The Weirs
3. Anchor Inn
4. White Bridge
5. Blunts Lane
6. Anchor Lane
7. Barcombe Mills

Walk 3

BARCOMBE MILLS

Distance	Approx. 4 miles.
Route	Pikes Bridge — The Weirs — Anchor Inn — White Bridge — Blunts Lane — Anchor Lane — Barcombe Mills — Pikes Bridge.
Maps	O/S Pathfinder 1289.
Start/Parking	The turning to Barcombe is off the A26 Lewes to Uckfield road. A car park is adjacent to Pikes Bridge.
Public Transport	Southdown Buses, 728, Lewes to Uckfield.
Conditions	A very easy, level walk, with several, wide well kept footbridges to cross.
Refreshments	Anchor Inn, Barcombe.

This quiet, unspoilt river walk starts on the fringe of Barcombe Mills, then wanders along the banks of the River Ouse which twists and turns and has so many side streams that one seems to be forever crossing little bridges. The meadows that abut the river are edged with willows and filled with a variety of buttercups in the summer. Many uncommon birds and occasionally, squirrels can be seen whilst cattle graze idly in the surrounding pastures. The walk itself does a sort of figure of eight, the meeting point in the middle being the lovely old Anchor Inn, built in 1790 and having gardens that run down to the river edge. This of course means you can stop for refreshments either going, coming back or perhaps both.

Barcombe Mills itself is beautiful, fascinating and historically complex. At one time there was a mill and horse drawn barges came this way. Now there is trout and coarse fishing, the scenery to enjoy, the weir to listen to, and the history to try and unravel. Further down the road, about five minutes walk, is a railway station. The line once ran between Lewes and Uckfield but closed in the 1960's. For a number of years it looked desolate and sad. However, it has recently been taken over as a restaurant and, albeit for a different use, is looking good once more.

The Anchor Inn.

Upstream — from Pikes Bridge.

Route Directions

From the car park turn right across a small bridge, Pikes Bridge (1) is the next one. Turn right here, through the "Sussex squeeze gate" and the River Ouse will be on the left. Notice the Weirs (2) in the background. Proceed along the towpath, over a footbridge, past Barcombe reservoir, through the field then across another wooden footbridge. Keep to the left and follow the river. Cross the next bridge then turn into a farmyard area and bear left along a narrow footpath. The river will be on the right and the Anchor Inn (3), which comes into view at this point, lies ahead. On reaching the Anchor Inn, cross the bridge in front and turn left. The River Ouse will be on the left once more. After passing under an old railway bridge, walk through the meadows by the river for about three quarters of a mile. You can briefly see the spire of Isfield church and then Isfield itself. Go over the next bridge which, although there's not a trace of white on it, is called White Bridge (4).

Turn left again and make towards a bridge in the far right corner of the field. Having crossed it, turn left up rather a muddy slope. Now follow the line of trees which lead on to a hedgerow that borders a wide grassy lane, called Blunt's Lane (5). Carry on until reaching Anchor Lane (6) which, after turning left, will take you over the disused Lewes to Uckfield railway line, past the signalman's cottage, and back to The Anchor Inn.

Turn right and right again by the sluice gates, through the field and along the footpath to the previously mentioned farmyard. Turn right along the tarmac road for half a mile. At Mill Farm turn left between a converted timber barn and a garage. Keep on, past Barcombe House, until you see and hear the weirs, the river and the trout pool at the scenically beautiful Barcombe Mills (7). Return to the car park via Pikes Bridge.

Points of Interest

The Anchor Inn

This charming public house is one of the smallest in England and is set in one of the loveliest parts of rural Sussex. It lies on the banks of the River Ouse, four miles from Lewes. Built in 1790, it originally catered for bargees, whose horse drawn barges travelled from Newhaven to Slaugham. The cargoes they carried included the bricks used to build the Balcombe Viaduct for the railway in 1846.

In 1895, the innkeeper of The Anchor was caught for smuggling and his licence was confiscated. The property was then acquired by Sir William Grantham of Barcombe Place. He carried out some alterations to the building and incorporated several ships timbers. Examples of posts taken from old windjammers can be seen in the main porch, which has unusual carved uprights supporting it.

The licence to run The Anchor as an inn once more, was regained in 1963. It also has exclusive boating rights over an upstream stretch of the River Ouse. This extends to the "fish ladder falls". The boats are for hire from The Anchor Inn and a trip there and back takes a leisurely two hours.

Barcombe Mills

This delightful spot consists of some old cottages, a farm, some barns, Barcombe House and, at one time, a mill. They are positioned by the River Ouse and the maze of waterways that make up Barcombe Mills. The weir, the canals, the sluice gates and the trout pool are all man made. It is now a favourite haunt for anglers.

Many years ago it was a working river. The horse drawn barges being pulled towards the mill that was astride the main stream. The largest bridge overlooks the weir. This leaves the main river above the mill and rejoins it just below. It was cut so that water could by-pass the mill when power was not needed and is called a "head and tail stream".

On the downstream side is a grass covered mound. This is the site of the last mill that burned down in 1939. The miller, who owned the road as well, charged tolls. A copy of the tolls is still there for all to see and it reads —

" Carriage and Horse	1s 0d.
Four Wheels and one Horse	9d.
Two Wheels and one Horse	6d.
Wagon and Horses	1s 6d.
Motor Cars	1s 0d.
Steam Engines	2s 0d.
Motor Cycle & Side Car	3d. "

Beneath Pikes Bridge runs a short canal, joining the loop of the main river. Exceptionally high tides reach here and barges had to be raised about 20 feet. Two locks were installed, one upstream and one downstream. These are now fish ladders and you can actually see the trout leap, one step at a time.

Barcombe Mills

Walk 4

DITCHLING BEACON

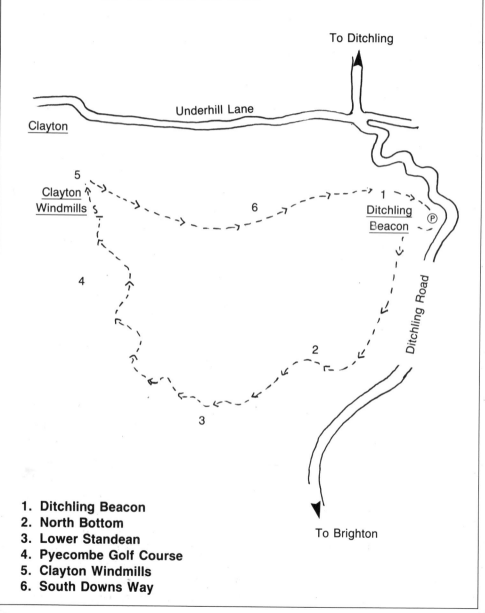

1. Ditchling Beacon
2. North Bottom
3. Lower Standean
4. Pyecombe Golf Course
5. Clayton Windmills
6. South Downs Way

Walk 4

DITCHLING BEACON

Distance	Approx. 5½ miles.
Route	Ditchling Beacon — North Bottom — Lower Standean — Pyecombe Golf Course — Clayton Windmills — South Downs Way — Ditchling Beacon.
Maps	O/S Pathfinder 1288.
Start/Parking	Ditchling Beacon Car Park, sited off the Brighton to Ditchling road about two miles south of Ditchling.
Public Transport	No public transport. Infrequent services to Ditchling Village only.
Conditions	A fairly dry walk across downland, with several relatively easy ascents.
Refreshments	The Jack and Jill, Clayton.

This breathtaking walk, starting on the highest point of the South Downs, should be done on a clear cloudless day, for the views are out of this world. One can see for miles across both East and West Sussex, across to the North Downs and then to the sea glittering in a distance. What a superb start to a beautiful walk. Because the views from Ditchling Beacon itself are so amazing, the immediate area can be busy at weekends, but one very soon leaves the car park and its occupants behind and is strolling in splendid isolation across the Downs. Isolation that is, except for large flocks of sheep with their lambs bleating continuously, looking curious and edging a little closer, only to beat a hasty retreat as 'Mama' moves ponderously away. Cattle, sitting in the shade, chewing the cud, indifferent and too lazy to move. A number of pheasants squawk noisily then disappear into the bushes. A dog barks from a nearby farm and the ever-present skylarks constantly sing.

"Don't look now, but I think we're being photographed".
Cattle grazing, near Ditchling Beacon.

So we move on through the countryside into a valley, then onto the Downs, which become noticeably more wooded as they stretch into West Sussex. A part of this walk actually slips into West Sussex, but it is such a splendid circular trail, that it would have been a pity not to bend the invisible boundaries just a little and include it in East Sussex.

Route Directions

Leave the Car Park at Ditchling Beacon (1) by the westward path. Cross the stile and carry on a short distance until reaching an information board about the Nature Reserve, on the right and a stile and a gate opposite. Turn left and follow the bridleway that will lead gently down the hill and along a valley. Still continuing down, pass through a field and a gate at the end of it into North Bottom (2). There are sheep and cattle grazing here, so dogs need to be kept on a lead. Now keep to the right and almost at the end of North Bottom is a gate besides a water trough. Turn right here and traverse the side of the hill to the next gate. This track lies just behind Lower Standean (3). Go through the gate and turn left. At the end of the slope, turn right and follow the bridleway up the hill, which turns to the left behind a small barn. Pass through the next two gates and turn sharp right up a small slope and make for the signs sited a little further on the right. On reaching them, notice that here is the Sussex Border Path, so having gone through the gate and turned left to follow the fence, you will now briefly be walking in West Sussex. It was just at this point, whilst stopping to contemplate the scenery, I noticed a four leaf clover at my feet and after a little searching two more were found. It was a very pleasant, unusual and hopefully lucky way of passing a few idle moments.

At the end of the field turn right onto a bridleway.

In the distance you can now see the two windmills. At the next gate turn left then take the first right and proceed past Pyecombe Golf Course (4) and follow the bridleway down to Clayton Windmills (5). If you wish to go down into Clayton for refreshments, make for the car park in front of the mills and in the far corner is a kissing gate and a signed footpath down to the village. It takes about ten minutes to get there.

Having viewed "Jack and Jill", rejoin the bridlepath and return up the hill but this time pass through an iron gate and progress eastwards. This is the South Downs Way (6). Continue for about two miles across the top of the Downs and back to Ditchling Beacon Car Park.

Points of Interest

Ditchling Beacon

At 814 ft high, Ditchling Beacon is the highest point of the South Downs. This was one of the beacons that used to be lit to warn of forthcoming marauders. It could be seen from Seaford to the North Downs. The hill is circled by traces of ramparts. Evidence suggests that this was an Iron Age hill fort, possibly about 2000 years old. The north slopes, at one time, were quarried for chalk and the series of pits can be seen below the South Downs Way. The whole area is now a nature reserve.

To Ditchling Beacon — To Clayton.

The East Sussex Panorama

The view, spread out before you, from Ditchling Beacon, looks like an enormous area of rolling patchwork. To the south lies Brighton, Hove and Shoreham, all merging into one, with the sea providing a background. Next to Brighton, perched on a hilltop is the racecourse and the Newmarket Hills. In the distance is Seaford Head. Situated in the east is Mount Caburn, Firle Beacon and beyond, Windover Hill and the downs on which you are standing, culminate in a valley at Lewes.

Clayton Windmills

These two windmills are known as Jack and Jill. Jack is a larger, brick tower mill, built in 1866 and worked until 1906. It is now privately owned. Jill is a fascinating example of a timbered post mill.

Originally built in Brighton in 1821, she was then transported, by oxen, to her present site in 1852. Like Jack she ceased milling in 1906, but in recent years, she has been completely restored and is now open to the public on Sunday afternoons.

Clayton Windmills.

Clayton

The pretty village of Clayton is tucked at the foot of the Downs, beneath the windmills. It has a most interesting church of Saxon origin with some fascinating wall paintings that could date from the 12th century.

Walk 5

RODMELL AND TELSCOMBE

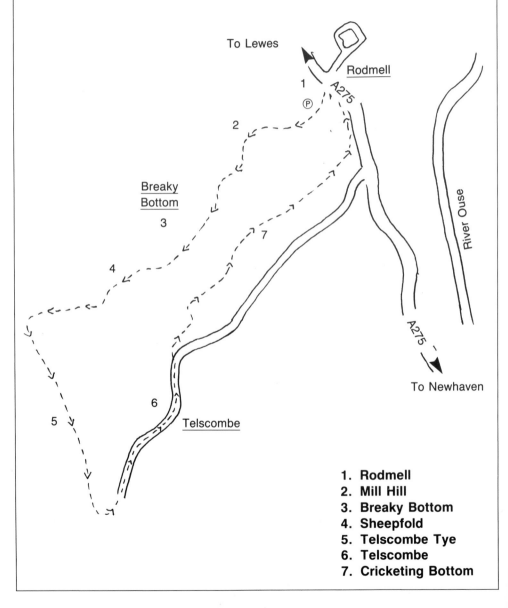

To Lewes

Rodmell

1

A275

P

2

Breaky Bottom

3

4

Breaky Bottom

7

River Ouse

A275

To Newhaven

6

Telscombe

5

1. Rodmell
2. Mill Hill
3. Breaky Bottom
4. Sheepfold
5. Telscombe Tye
6. Telscombe
7. Cricketing Bottom

Walk 5

RODMELL AND TELSCOMBE

Distance	Approx. 5½ miles.
Route	Rodmell — Mill Hill — Breaky Bottom — Sheepfold — Telscombe Tye — Telscombe — Cricketing Bottom — Rodmell.
Maps	O/S Pathfinder 1307 and Pathfinder 1308.
Start/Parking	Rodmell Village. Sited either side of the A275 Lewes to Newhaven road.
Public Transport	Southdown Buses, 123.
Conditions	A hilly walk and therefore it can be windy. A part of the return journey is, however, through a sheltered valley.
Refreshments	The Abergavenny Arms, Rodmell.

This particular walk is not for the faint hearted. It starts gently enough, in the pretty village of Rodmell, but in the open countryside it soon becomes "up hill and down dale" terrain, old flint walls still occasionally dividing the large fields. It is a classic ramble for seeing sweeping expanses of the bare but beautiful East Sussex Downs, with wonderful views, eventually culminating at Brighton and Saltdean, the sea clearly visible on the horizon.

Many years ago, large flocks of sheep grazed here and in the valley, on the return journey, are some flint farm buildings, still partially used, with an old shepherd's hut, wedged and forgotten, against one exterior wall. The tranquil hamlet of Telscombe is completely hidden until one is directly above it, on Telscombe Tye. It is nicely sheltered from the strong winds that can blow in with a vengeance from the coast across the surrounding hills, which are more than 200 feet above sea level.

Mill Hill at Rodmell, stands higher than the others, and as we wind our way back, below it, the countryside imperceptibly changes. Gone is that timeless, exciting feeling of exploring rather wild and solitary downland. Slowly, it is replaced by hedgerows, cottages and the distant hum of traffic, as one returns to Rodmell.

Telscombe Church.

Route Directions

The walk starts in Rodmell (1) itself, at the lane leading between the small garage on the A275 and the White House. Carry on up the lane until reaching a gate at the very top. This is Mill Hill (2). Keep straight on southwestwards, down the hill and up the other side. Now, on the right, tucked in the valley, is the Breaky Bottom Vineyard (3). Continue through the next two gates and keeping the fence to the left, go down to the old sheepfold (4), built in flint. Still keeping the fence on the left, cross the field to the next gate, then up the hill and turn left at the bridleway. This is Telscombe Tye (5). Proceed straight on through the fields (ignore the path that goes to the left), until reaching a narrow country road. Turn left and this will lead down into Telscombe (6). From Telscombe Tye there are amazing, far reaching views, including across to Seaford Bay and Seaford Head in the east.

Pass through the quaint old village of Telscombe along the road and up the hill. At the top, bear left on a bridleway that descends down the side of the hill and along a valley called Cricketing Bottom (7). Walk through the valley which weaves in and out of the downland for about two miles until reaching the main A275. Turn left along the wide grass verge and back into Rodmell.

Points of Interest

Breaky Bottom

The first modern vineyard in England was planted in 1951. Breaky Bottom is just one of the 350 vineyards that are now spread over southern England, many of which are in the south-east. It lies in a sheltered valley near Rodmell and produces some excellent English wine. The vineyard is open to the public.

Telscombe

An unspoilt village, nestling in the folds of the Downs. It has no tea room, shop or public house, so it is not for the hordes of tourists. There is a large stud farm and it was from these stables, eighty years ago, that a horse won the Grand National. The trainer was Ambrose Gorham. He subsequently purchased the surrounding land and on his death in 1933, bequeathed his estate to the Brighton Corporation. The flint manor house has a rather strange circular tower and opposite, on raised ground, stands the church, having a Norman nave, an early English tower, a 13th century font and beautiful stained glass windows. Most of the old barns have been tastefully converted, but they still retain all their original charm and therefore, do not detract from the peaceful atmosphere of Telscombe.

Rodmell

A very picturesque village, having an assortment of enchanting properties, dating from various centuries, with typically English gardens. It has become increasingly popular over the last few years and a number of new houses have been built. The old part lies on the eastern side of the main road and borders onto the marshes, or the 'brooks', as it is called, that lie on either side of the River Ouse.

For some years, Leonard and Virginia Woolf made their home in Monks House, a converted farmhouse, just near the church. The property, which still contains some of their furniture and personal items, has been acquired by the National Trust and is open to visitors.

Monks House, Rodmell. Home of Leonard and Virginia Woolf.

Telscombe villiage

Walk 6

JEVINGTON AND WILMINGTON

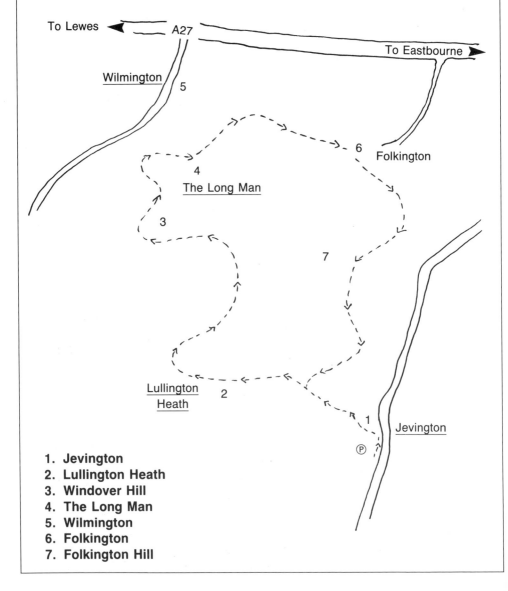

1. Jevington
2. Lullington Heath
3. Windover Hill
4. The Long Man
5. Wilmington
6. Folkington
7. Folkington Hill

Walk 6

JEVINGTON AND WILMINGTON

Distance	Approx. 6¾ miles.
Route	Jevington — Lullington Heath — Windover Hill — The Long Man — Wilmington — Folkington — Folkington Hill — Jevington.
Maps	O/S Pathfinder 1324.
Start/Parking	By Jevington Church. In the Car Park at the southern end of Jevington Village. The road to Jevington runs between the A27 and the A259, west of Eastbourne.
Public Transport	Local Rider 213 to Jevington. Southdown Buses, 726 to Wilmington.
Conditions	Quite a lot of climbing and some of the bridleways could be churned up and muddy after rain. Can be quite cold and windy across Lullington Heath and Windover Hill.
Refreshments	Eight Bells Inn, Jevington. The Giants Rest, Wilmington.

This is probably the longest and one of the most scenic walks in the book, but it is possibly the most tiring as there is quite a lot of climbing and the terrain is varied. However, the very beautiful scenery is worth all the effort.

It is an ideal walk to do for a day and maybe stop off at Wilmington, not only for lunch, but to explore the old village, the old priory and the church which boasts a yew tree that is over a thousand years old. Arrive back in Jevington in time for refreshments at The Eight Bells. Incidentally, do not try and reach The Eight Bells on foot along the road. There is no pavement and a sharp corner, so it could be dangerous. Instead, follow the path by St. Andrew's Church, through the churchyard and old tapsell gate then past Jevington Place. The pub will now be immediately ahead of you.

The bridleway from Wilmington to Jevington is part of the old turnpike road, the route stagecoaches used around 1750 to 1820 from Lewes to Eastbourne. Somehow it's not hard to let the imagination travel back to that era and visualize a stagecoach, the horses foaming at the mouth, galloping along, with autumn leaves falling on an evening that has a hint of early winter chill.

There is a tremendous variety in the landscape on this circular walk. At Folkington and Jevington there are woods, sheltering against the northern slopes of the Downs, filled with bluebells in April and May, then later in the clearings, foxgloves. For the bird watcher, an assortment of birds can be seen, such as woodpeckers, buntings, meadow pipits, nightingales, jays and one must never forget the downland favourites, skylarks and kestrels. At Lullington Heath and Windover Hill, which is over 700 feet above sea level, you have the high wide open spaces and magnificent views, then on reaching the Long Man, which is more sheltered, there are cornfields, narrow lanes and high banks with hedges of hawthorn, hazel and elder, leading back towards Folkington.

Windover Hill — from the west.

Route Directions

On leaving the car park at the southerly end of Jevington (1), turn left on to the main road, taking the next left into Church Lane and make for St. Andrew's Church, noticing its Saxon tower dated 900-950.

Keeping the church on the right, follow the track leading up into the woods. The gnarled roots of the trees almost seem to act as steps. Carry on directly through the woods until the track ends. Turn left along the bridleway. At the top of the hill take the left fork of the bridleway. A short distance on is Lullington Heath Nature Reserve (2). An information board marks the entrance and there is also a warning about heath fires. As you walk on there are some beautiful views, Friston Forest on the left, in the distance the sea, Cuckmere Haven and Seaford. To the right Firle Beacon and Mount Caburn, near Lewes.

At the next hilltop there is a crossing of bridleways, turn right and follow the signed way to the Long Man.

After leaving the Nature Reserve, go through the next two gates then keep to the path for three quarters of a mile. It does a half loop back on itself before arriving at the top of Windover Hill (3). Descend the hill about two thirds of the way then bear right down a narrow track and go through the next gate on the right.

Now traverse the Downs until reaching the Long Man (4) which will be on the right. Go down past the dewpond to the information board about The Long Man.

Should you wish to stop in Wilmington (5), which you can see from this point, the way is marked and takes about fifteen minutes.

Continue traversing the Downs northeastwards, past a small copse, keeping the fence to the left, then climb up towards the woodland. Descend into the wood itself, through a small gate and turn right onto the bridleway. This was the old turnpike road. Proceed down to Folkington Church and Village (6) turning right by the church. Take the track along the left side of the field and into a wide, flower filled lane. It is a very easy path to follow and bears right round Folkington Hill (7).

Continue for about a mile, turn right, ignoring the sign to Jevington on the left, this would bring you out at the northern end of the village. Take the next left and retrace your steps through the wood and past St. Andrew's Church to Jevington.

Points of Interest

Jevington

A charming unspoilt village in the folds of the Downs and like other Sussex villages is of Saxon origin. In fact its church must be one of the few that can claim a Saxon tower dating from the 10th century. It has extremely thick walls and two bells, one dated 1470. Opposite the church is a field known as "Monastery Field". Here lie the foundations of an early monks' settlement dedicated to St. Lewinna.

An interesting collection of properties, dating from the 15th century, make up the village. The Old Manor House, Jevington Place, is listed in the Domesday Book. What is now The Hungry Monk Restaurant, used to be the home of the infamous smuggler, Jevington Jig. The old school, a village hall now, is high on the bank opposite Jevington Place. The Eight Bells Inn has an underground tunnel, once used by smugglers, leading to King's Farthing opposite. This was originally three cottages. A selection of old barns, Street Farm, the old Post Office, now a private house, they all help to make Jevington a most delightful place to visit.

Lullington Heath

This nature reserve was established in 1954 and is one of the largest areas of chalk heath remaining in Britain. It is leased from The Forestry Commission who manage the adjoining Friston Forest. In the areas of the plentiful yellow gorse, there is numerous wildlife and both foxes and badgers breed in the shelter of the scrub. The occasional adder has also been seen but, if left undisturbed, they are harmless. In the summer, butterflies, such as marbled whites, chalk hill blue, brimstone and fritillary hover on the downland flowers. Six different species of orchid have been recorded. These include the early purple, spotted and bee orchid.

To the west of the reserve is a long barrow. This indicates that these Downs were inhabited between 3000-1800 BC by neolithic settlers. In 1927 excavations revealed pottery belonging to the late Bronze or early Iron Age (500-250 BC). Aerial photos taken before the scrub grew show a Celtic field system of terracing called "Lynchets". The tilling of these little square fields probably continued until the arrival of the Saxon plough in the 5th century.

The Long Man.

The Long Man

Historians are still unsure of the age of The Long Man or why he was put there. He is approximately 226 feet high and the first records show him holding a scythe and a rake rather than staves.

There is a possibility he could have been carved during neolithic times. Or he could have been carved to indicate the 13th century Benedictine priory at Wilmington. Whatever, this huge chalk figure conveyed something and certainly was meant to be seen for many miles around. Maybe, one day, somebody will find the answer.

Folkington.

Wilmington

A pretty village, tucked beneath the Downs, consisting mainly of one long lane, a pub, a lovely old church and the remains of a 13th century priory. This is owned by The Sussex Archaeological Society and is open to the public.

St. Andrew's Church, Jevington

The Hungry Monk Restaurant, Jevington

Walk 7

FIRLE

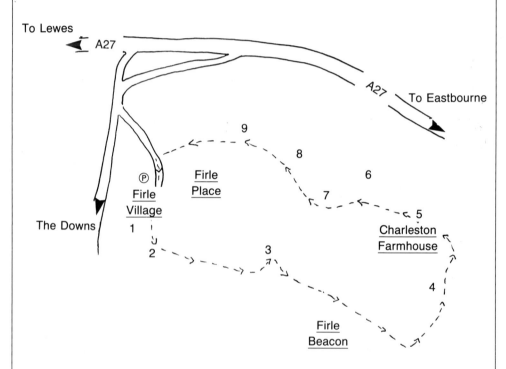

To Lewes

A27

To Eastbourne

9

8

6

Firle
Place

7

(P)

Firle
Village

5

Charleston
Farmhouse

The Downs

1

2

3

4

Firle
Beacon

1. **Firle Village**
2. **Place Farm**
3. **Beanstalk**
4. **Tilton Farm**
5. **Charleston Farmhouse**
6. **Compton Wood**
7. **Firle Tower**
8. **Heighton Street**
9. **West Firle**

Walk 7

FIRLE

Distance	Approx. 4 miles.
Route	Firle Village — Place Farm — Beanstalk — Tilton Farm — Charleston Farm — Compton Wood — Firle Tower — Heighton Street — West Firle — Firle Village.
Maps	O/S Pathfinder 1308.
Start/Parking	Firle Village. Just off the A27, about 3 miles East of Lewes.
Public Transport	Brighton and Eastbourne Buses, 30.
Conditions	An easy walk with no steep slopes, but the bridleway at the foot of the Downs can be very muddy.
Refreshments	The Ram Inn, Firle Village.

It is essential to spend some time in the charming village of Firle as there is plenty to see. Firle is a fine example of an old tied village, the manor to which it was tied, being Firle Place. To this day, many of the locals still work on the Firle estate.

The attractive walk from Firle initially follows part of the old turnpike road that ran between Lewes and Eastbourne until 1812, when it closed, therefore making Firle a cul-de-sac. In the summer the downland is peppered with the pungent wild thyme and the bridleways are flanked either side, first with white hedge parsley, then with wild campion.

Several spectacular beech trees stand at the foot of Firle Beacon, the highest Down in this particular range. Unfortunately one of the trees has been struck by lightning, giving it a somewhat deformed appearance.

On the return walk, the track moves away from the Downs and passes through lush green fields, skirts a woodland which is home to bluebells in the spring, and finally meanders through the magnificent parkland of West Firle before returning to Firle Village.

Firle Place.

Firle Beacon.

Route Directions

Walk through Firle Village (1) keeping the church on the left. Continue along the side of the rather untidy farmyard called Place Farm (2). After passing the farmyard, take the bridleway to the left. This leads along the foot of the Downs. After half a mile, there is a left hand turning. Ignore this but pause to notice the selection of fine old beech trees, before continuing along the foot of the Downs. After a quarter of a mile the track bends to the left by the unusual Beanstalk (3) cottage and it then returns to the right again. Here you will see a fine view of Firle Tower. Keep on the bridleway with the Downs on the right and the Weald of Sussex spread out on the left. About a mile further on you will see two separate lots of farm buildings. Keep on until you reach the furthest buildings, then turn left, down past Tilton Farm (4).

Once past Tilton Farm turn left again up the concrete path towards Charleston Farmhouse (5). Although on this return walk there are occasionally signs indicating the way, there is not a well marked footpath, so do follow the route directions carefully.

On reaching Charleston Farmhouse, look at the old pond and garden fronting this lovely Sussex farmhouse, now famous because Vanessa Bell lived there.

Keeping the house on the right, go through the gate ahead leading into a field. Compton Woods (6) will be on the right. At the end of the field, on the left, is another gate; go through this, turn right immediately across a small stream and up to the next gate. Having gone through this, traverse the side of the hill with Firle Tower (7) on the right. Tucked in a small coppice of trees is yet another gate which takes you into a field and down to some cottages. On reaching the cottages you will find a tumble down gateway; go through this and almost straight away go through a second iron gate, adjacent to one of the houses. You will now be in Heighton Street (8) which, in spite of its name, is only a bridleway.

Opposite the cottages is the entrance to West Firle (9), an area of parkland belonging to Firle Place, owned by Lord Gage. Follow the unmade track on the right, through the park with the magnificent Firle Place on the left. At this point there is an excellent view of it. The track finishes at a gateway and the short lane beyond leads back into Firle Village. The village store and Post Office are at the top of the lane on the right and the church is on the left.

Points of Interest

Firle Village

The Firle estate is owned by the Gage family. The Gages have been in Firle since the 15th century and although the records are somewhat fragmentary, a history of them can be found in Firle Place.

The lovely church was built in the 13th century. The aisle arcades and the vestry were added in the 14th and 15th centuries. In 1985 a 'John Piper' window was installed in memory of the sixth Viscount Gage, KCVO.

During the 18th century extensive alterations were carried out on Firle Place leaving it much as you see it today. During this time the agricultural trade flourished and Firle like other villages prospered. Georgian houses were added alongside the old flint cottages and there were four public houses, one of them being the Beanstalk on the old turnpike road. Now only the Ram is left. A village school was built and Firle possessed a miller, a tailor, a baker, a saddler, a blacksmith and a shoemaker. Life has changed dramatically today but the village has barely altered and as you walk through, it almost seems that time has passed it pleasantly by.

Firle Beacon

Firle Beacon is more than 700ft high . This prominent stretch of downland commands spectacular views northwards across the Weald of Sussex and southwards to the coastline and English Channel.

A long time ago fires (beacons) were lit from the cliff top and on the highest point of the Downs stretching inland. This was to warn people that invaders were approaching the English coast. Hence the name Firle Beacon. It is possible to deviate on this walk and by using the signed "South Downs Way", it will take you across the top of Firle Beacon. However, it is much longer and the climb is fairly strenuous.

Charleston Farmhouse

Vanessa Bell, Virginia Woolf's sister, bought Charleston Farmhouse in 1916. Vanessa, herself an artist, moved in with the painter Duncan Grant and the writer David Garnett. Together they made up a part of the now famous "Bloomsbury Set". Well known names visited Charleston during the twenties and thirties, such as: Roger Fry, T. S. Eliot, Maynard Keynes, Lytton Strachey and E. M. Forster.

Charleston Farmhouse.

The farmhouse itself is a fascinating extension of both Vanessa's and Duncan's personalities and, of course those who visited. They were all artists in various forms and they all contributed to both the interior and exterior of the house and garden. Pictures and murals were painted, ceramics and pottery made, unique wallpapers and textiles were designed; even some of the furniture was made and decorated and the woodwork in the house painted in varying colours.

Vanessa and Duncan lived on at Charleston until their deaths, respectively in the sixties and seventies. The house is now in the care of the Charleston Trust and is open to the public.

Firle Place

Firle Place nestles at the foot of the South Downs set in scenic parkland. It is home to the Gage family and has been so since the 15th century. The original Tudor manor house was built of Caen stone, but was the subject of extensive alterations in the 18th century. Records show that, although the size of the property did not change much, the entire north-east front was rebuilt giving it the early Georgian appearance we now see. The house, which is open to the public, contains important European and English old master paintings, a fine collection of French and English furniture and English and French porcelain, including Sevres.

Walk 8

ARLINGTON

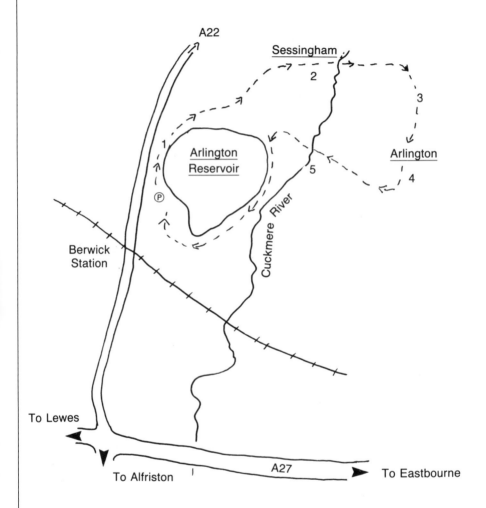

1. **Arlington Reservoir**
2. **Sessingham Farm**
3. **Raylands Farm**
4. **Arlington Village**
5. **Cuckmere River**

Walk 8

ARLINGTON

Distance	Approx. 3¾ miles.
Route	Arlington Reservoir — Sessingham Farm — Raylands Farm — Arlington Village — Cuckmere River — Arlington Reservoir.
Maps	O/S Pathfinder 1308.
Start/Parking	Arlington Reservoir. Half a mile from Berwick Station. One and a half miles from the A27 at Drusillas roundabout.
Public Transport	British Rail to Berwick Station. Cuckmere Community Bus.
Conditions	A level and easy walk with one or two narrow footbridges to cross.
Refreshments	Yew Tree Inn, Arlington.

The fact that part of this walk covers the perimeter of a man made reservoir, does not detract in any way from the enjoyable scenery. In many ways, it adds another different aspect to the Sussex Weald, especially as the area around Arlington Reservoir has been beautifully landscaped and is also a Nature Reserve.

After about half a mile, the bridleway moves into more traditional English countryside. The farmed fields being edged with streams, the banks scattered with primroses, anemones and catkins. During the summer, the fields themselves are full of corn and frequently have an abundance of red poppies mingling with the golden ears. The River Cuckmere is crossed twice. The first time, its rather overgrown, narrow banks will belie that when crossed a second time, just a little further downstream, it is wide with gracious curves and fringed with willows.

Throughout this walk the Downs will provide a pleasing backdrop, from Firle Beacon in the West, to Windover in the East.

The River Cuckmere.

Arlington Reservoir.

Route Directions

On leaving the car park and picnic area, take the signed footpath to the left along the edge of Arlington Reservoir (1). This becomes a bridleway and after half a mile bears left, away from the footpath and reservoir. Carry on through the gate and the next two fields, keeping the hedge on the left. Three are some rather ugly pylons here, that mar this part of a very pleasant walk. Sessingham Farm (2) will now come into view on the left. Just past Sessingham farmhouse, which is semi-derelict, is a very narrow footbridge. Having crossed it, turn right and continue on the gravel track until the next, much larger footbridge. This crosses the Cuckmere for the first time. If you look up river at this point, it is possible to distinguish the overgrown moated site of Sessingham. Keep on the bridleway, past Raylands Farm (3), then immediately turn sharp right, along the almost invisibly signed footpath to Arlington. Now go across the next two stiles, through the gate and then to the left, keeping the trees on your right. Follow the track through the middle of the next field towards Arlington Church. Cross the stile that leads into the old churchyard. On leaving by the kissing gates, you will be in Arlington (4). Should you want to pause for a while on this walk, explore the village and stop for refreshments at the Yew Tree Inn, then turn left. Otherwise turn right from the church.

Having crossed the stile, go through the field to the next stile and turn right. Make for the modern bridge that crosses the Cuckmere River (5) for the second time, up the hill, turn left and go along the path by the eastern side of the reservoir. Turn right and walk behind Polshill Farm before returning to the reservoir. Follow the marked way back to the car park.

Points of Interest

Arlington Reservoir

Arlington Reservoir, which covers about 120 acres, was designed by the East Sussex County Council as a local nature reserve. It was completed by Eastbourne Water Company in 1971 and supplies all the local areas. It is also a private trout fly fishery. The reservoir itself was formed by blocking a meander in the River Cuckmere with a dam. The surrounds have been planted with 30,000 trees including oak, birch, wild cherry, hazel, willow, mountain ash and hawthorn.

The area is noted by the Nature Conservancy Council as a site of special scientific interest because of its value to wintering birds. Over a hundred and seventy different species have so far been recorded.

Sessingham

The area eastwards past Sessingham Farm is almost certainly the region of Sessingham listed in Domesday, when it had a watermill and a population of fifty. The river divides here to form a small naturally moated island. It is possible, when standing on the footbridge and looking upstream, to identify this moat. The track called Tye Hill Road which leads from Arlington to Sessingham, was once used by horses and carriages. As late as 1893 surveyors were requested to "repair the horsebridge at Sessingham".

Arlington

This is a rambling village with a very good public house called The Yew Tree Inn, interesting properties, some of them Tudor and a Saxon church. At one time there was an old Clergy House but this was demolished about 1850, when a new vicarage was built a short distance away. Foundations of medieval structures and some medieval pottery were uncovered in the grounds of the old school house and there are indications that nearby lies the site of an old Roman village, who knows, perhaps the first Arlington.

The church itself is built of flint and is of Saxon origin, although the main part, built at a later date, is probably Norman. There are clear remains of wall paintings and some work has been carried out on these. In 1889, the Bishop of Chichester described the church as being in a "state of ruin, dirt and decay, worse than any other church in Sussex". Thereupon, the young newly appointed Reverend Thomas Bunston set about the raising of funds for its restoration, including the siting of a new school. At this point in time the chapel was being used as a schoolroom. The Rev. Bunston was successful in his efforts to bring the church back to its former glory and after he died in 1916, a tablet to his memory and achievements was put up in the chancel.

Swans on the River Cuckmere

Walk 9

GLYNDE AND MOUNT CABURN

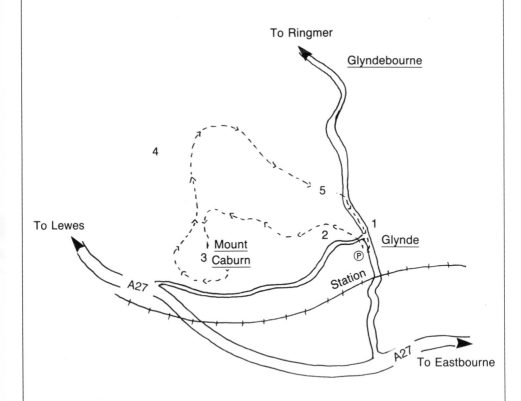

1. **Glynde**
2. **Ranscombe Lane**
3. **Mount Caburn**
4. **Caburn Bottom**
5. **Home Farm**

Walk 9

GLYNDE AND MOUNT CABURN

Distance	Approx. 3 miles.
Route	Glynde — Ranscombe Lane — Mount Caburn — Caburn Bottom — Home Farm — Glynde.
Maps	O/S Pathfinder 1308.
Start/Parking	Glynde, just off the A27, about two miles east of Lewes. Parking near the old Post Office or the railway station.
Public Transport	British Rail to Glynde Station.
Conditions	A long rather arduous climb up to Mount Caburn but the incredible views are worth the effort.
Refreshments	The Trevor Arms, Glynde.

This is not a long circular walk, but it should be done on a clear fine day as the views from the top of Mount Caburn, the downland behind Glynde Village, are amongst the most panoramic in Sussex. It makes the long climb worth every step.

Looking southeastwards from this splendid vantage point, are Itford Hill and Firle Beacon, Caburn's counterpart on the opposite side of the valley. Ahead lies the area of marshland that borders the River Ouse. The river mouth at Newhaven can be seen in the distance. The downland to the west stretches towards Brighton and at the foot of the facing slopes are some delightful villages. To the northwest, barely visible, lies Lewes, the river like a silver snake, winding towards it. From Mount Caburn one can walk to Lewes, over the Downs, then past the golf course and descend a steep lane that leads to the old Cliffe High Street.

It would of course be perfectly possible to park at Lewes, then take the train to Glynde and return via the Downs. Below Mount Caburn is the A27, Lewes to Eastbourne road. The traffic, seemingly noiseless from this height, looks like an assortment of beetles crawling along a track. This is not a walk to be hurried over. Spend some time and enjoy the atmosphere that pervades the Sussex Downs.

Entrance to Glynde Place.

Route Directions

Having parked the car in Glynde (1), make your way to the old Post Office in Ranscombe Lane (2), at the centre of this tiny village. Cross the stile opposite the Post Office and follow the track up across the field to the next stile. Now the walk becomes fairly tiring as it is a long, continuous and quite steep climb. Believe me, it's worth it. Proceed until reaching the top of the ascent and the next stile. Do not cross it, turn left instead towards Mount Caburn (3). At the gate, which is the entrance to the Mount Caburn Nature Reserve, is an area information board. Spend some time exploring this old Iron Age hill fort, it's fascinating, then linger awhile to enjoy the views. Now retrace your steps back to the entrance of this nature reserve and continue to follow the fence on the left. Should you want to extend the walk, now is the time to do so. The Downs stretch for several miles in three directions and as Mount Caburn provides a good landmark, you will not lose the way.

The valley in the centre of the downland on the left is Caburn Bottom (4). At the next iron gateway, turn right down the chalk track. Follow this downhill path for about three quarters of a mile, it is lined with cowslips, passes a copse full of bluebells and an old quarry that has a profusion of wild violets. On leaving the bottom of the track, look to the left, in the distance one can just make out the chimneys of the famous Glyndebourne Opera House. At the foot of the Downs is Home Farm (5), bear left here, then immediately right, back into Glynde.

Points of Interest

Mount Caburn

This curiously ridged hill top was in fact an Iron Age fort and dates from 500 BC. It is fortified by a ditch and rampart with a second rampart to the north, added about AD 43. The whole area is now a nature reserve and wild orchids, rampion, marjoram and cowslips are among the flowers that flourish on these Downs.

Glyndebourne

This fine old Tudor Manor lies north of Glynde Village. The famous adjacent Opera House, built in 1934 by John Christie is now in the process of being rebuilt on an even grander scale. It is a fairytale setting for any opera and its audience.

Glynde

Glynde is a small, mainly flint built village, with a population of about two hundred. Originally, most of the cottages were used to house the workers from the Glynde Estates. Even today, a large proportion of the villagers still work on the estate and rent those same cottages. Property rarely comes on the market here and when it does, it is highly sought after.

There are several interesting buildings in Glynde and one is certainly the Smithy with a most unusual horseshoe shaped facade. Nearby is the old school and a lovely rambling timber framed house. The Georgian vicarage boasts two fire insurance plaques and on a sloping hillside stands the Georgian church. It adjoins the magnificent Elizabethan flint mansion, Glynde Place. Built in the 16th century, it overlooks beautiful parkland and has been lived in by several Sussex families including Morleys, Trevors and Brands. It is now owned by Lord Hampden, whose family have been in the village since 1824. It is open to the public during the summer season.

In the churchyard is a tomb to John Ellman, the 'inventor' of the Southdown breed of sheep. At the southern end of Glynde is The Trevor Arms and the tiny railway station, with frequent services to Lewes and Eastbourne.

Glynde Church.

Village Stores and Post Office, Glynde

Stile, Mount Caburn. Looking towards Glynde

Walk 10

THE CUCKOO LINE

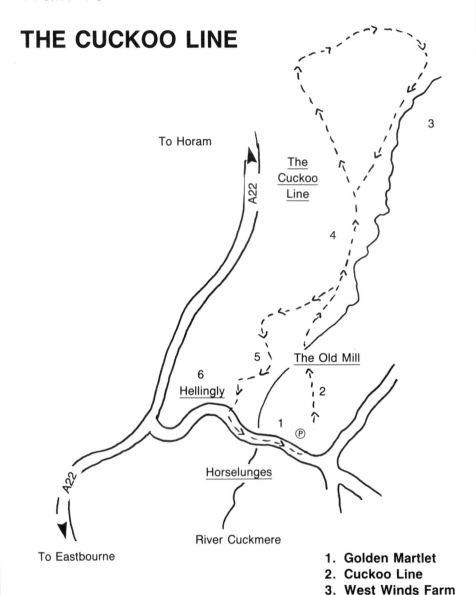

To Horam

A22

The
Cuckoo
Line

3

4

The Old Mill

5

6
Hellingly

2

1 ℗

Horselunges

A22

To Eastbourne

River Cuckmere

1. **Golden Martlet**
2. **Cuckoo Line**
3. **West Winds Farm**
4. **Cuckoo Line**
5. **Mill Lane**
6. **Hellingly**

Walk 10

THE CUCKOO LINE

Distance	Approx. 5 miles.
Route	Golden Martlet — Cuckoo Line — West Winds Farm — Cuckoo Line — Mill Lane — Hellingly — Golden Martlet.
Maps	O/S Pathfinder 1289.
Start/Parking	Golden Martlet Car Park. Hellingly.
Public Transport	Southdown Buses, 728. Local Rider 218.
Conditions	A level walk that could be very muddy after rain, especially on some footpaths by the river.
Refreshments	Golden Martlet Inn, Hellingly.

An enchanting, gentle and unassuming walk, taking in part of the Cuckoo Line, a disused railway track which is set amongst the rolling pastureland between Hellingly, Horsebridge and Horam. Here there are no sweeping aspects across the Sussex Weald, no glimpses of the sea and even the Downs are hidden from view. However, there is something different and rather unusual about following a footpath made for a railway. How many times has one peered through a grubby carriage window and thought, "Why is it there are more wild flowers on a railway embankment than anywhere else? If only one could walk this way, how lovely it would be"? Now you can. The railway lines have gone but the assortment of wild flowers, from small white anemones to tall pink foxgloves, are still there.

The latter part of the walk goes through a most attractive "Beatrix Potter" type woodland with a stream, then water meadows by the River Cuckmere, and briefly joins the Cuckoo Line again. Finally it passes through farmed pastures leading to the picturesque Hellingly Village.

Old Bridge on The Cuckoo Line.

Hellingly Church.

Route Directions

Leave the Golden Martlet (1) Car Park by the stile in the far corner. Turn left and immediately you are on the Cuckoo Line (2). Notice the old Hellingly station which is now a private residence, behind you. Proceed down the track, across a lane and carry on northwards passing first, The Old Mill at Hellingly on the left, then crossing the River Cuckmere. Continue until reaching a double arched railway bridge, which one can only assume was a passing point for trains. After the bridge are gates either side of the path. Walk on past these for about forty yards, turn right and go down through a "kissing gate".

Now cross the field to a stile and footbridge that leads up into a delightful woodland boasting a mass of woodland flowers. Go over the next stile and keeping the fence to the right, go through the gate at the end of the field and follow the track that bears left then right. At the bottom of the incline, turn left then right towards the gate at the end of the meadow, turn left and follow the River Cuckmere.

West Winds Farm (3) will be on the hill to the left of the river. Proceed through two fields, across a footbridge then rejoin the Cuckoo Line (4) from the gate at the end of the next field. Walk down the track for about three quaters of a mile until reaching some steps up to a stile on the right. Cross the stile, turn left, through a field and gate then across another field to a footbridge with a stile either side. Pass through the next two fields towards a farm. Now walk by the farmyard and farm, keeping them both to the right. The track here is muddy from cattle and ill-kept. A short untidy path at the side of the farmhouse leads into Mill Lane (5). Turn right here and proceed until reaching Hellingly (6) and the lovely old church. Turn left at the church, back towards the Golden Martlet.

Points of Interest

The Cuckoo Line

This railway which ran from Polegate to Heathfield and Eridge, acquired its name from the Sussex tradition of releasing a cuckoo every spring at the Heathfield Fair. The line was fully opened in 1880, but less than a hundred years later, it was a victim of the 1960's closures. The last freight service ran to Heathfield in 1968.

In 1981 Wealden District Council and the East Sussex County Council purchased the line south of Heathfield and allowed it to be used as a public trail. Now Wealden, together with Sustrans, a charity specializing in paths on disused railways, hope to provide and maintain a trail, not only for walkers, but for cyclists and horseriders as well.

The Old Mill

The beautiful old mill lies by the river at Hellingly and could possibly be on the site of the mill documented over 700 years ago. It claims to be the oldest watermill in England and was last used for milling in 1919. In the 1930's it was advertised as "The Old Watermill Tea Rooms". The mill has now been completely restored and the entire complex is privately owned.

Hellingly

Hellingly is a small village, dominated by a lovely square Norman church, opposite which, in the churchyard itself, is a semi-circle of very quaint old cottages. It is also the meeting place for the two headstreams of the Cuckmere, the sources being at Possingworth and Heathfield.

Horselunges

Having crossed the river, on the road back to the Golden martlet, is Horselunges. It is beautifully situated and a splendid example of a fifteenth century, timber framed, moated Manor House.

POINTS TO REMEMBER

1) Keep to public rights of way.

2) Fasten all gates.

3) Keep dogs under control.

4) Do not leave litter around.

5) Do not disturb cattle, sheep or other animals.

6) Do not pick wild flowers.

7) Leave the countryside as you find it so others can enjoy it too.

TRANSPORT AND INFORMATION

British Rail

Train times and fares – Tel (01273) 206755

Bus Services

Bus Helpline – Tel (01273) 478007

Tourist Information Centres

Brighton
10 Bartholomew Square
Tel (01273) 323755

Eastbourne
Cornfield Road
Tel (01323) 411400

Lewes
132 High Street
Tel (01273) 483448